Is That the New Moon?
Poems by Women Poets

When Wendy Cope's poetry collection, *Making Cocoa for Kingsley Amis*, was published, she was immediately established as one of Britain's foremost poets.

For this anthology of poems Wendy has chosen poems by women poets about their own and other women's experience. This is a collection of vibrant, funny, tender, sad and moving poems from the leading women poets of our time.

Wendy Cope (Ed)

Is That the New Moon?

Poems by Women Poets

with illustrations by
Christine Roche

LIONS · TEEN TRACKS

First published in Great Britain 1989 by
Lions Teen Tracks
8 Grafton Street, London W1X 3LA

Lions Teen Tracks is an imprint of
the Children's Division, part of
the Collins Publishing Group

Printed in Great Britain
by William Collins Sons & Co. Ltd, Glasgow

Contents

Acknowledgements

The publishers gratefully acknowledge permission to reprint copyright material to the following:

Oxford University Press for *Kissing* from **The Incident Book** by Fleur Adcock (1986); Oxford University Press for *Street Song* and *Things* from Fleur Adcock's **Selected Poems** (1983); Oxford University Press for *Incident* from **Minute by Glass Minute** by Anne Stevenson (1982); Oxford University Press for *Television* from Anne Stevenson's **Selected Poems 1956-1986**; Oxford University Press for *Girls' Talk* and Part 1 of *Between the Lines* from **Broken Moon** by Carol Satyamurti (1987); Virago for *Two Sketches* from **Beginning the Avocado** by Gillian Allnutt; Virago for *Still I Rise* from **And Still I Rise** by Maya Angelou; Virago for *Girl's Gifts* from **Kisses for Mayakovsky** by Alison Fell; Virago for *Peanut Vendor* from **Long Road to Nowhere** by Amryl Johnson; Virago for *Beauty* and *Like a Flame* from **The Fat Black Woman's Poems** by Grace Nichols; Jonathan Cape for *Late Night* from **True Stories** by Margaret Atwood; Dudley Russell for *Paul O'Chatberg Grogan* from **Bill Spink's Bedstead and Other Poems** by Pam Ayres; Elizabeth Bartlett for *God is Dead – Nietzsche* from **A Lifetime of Dying**, Peterloo Poets; Carcanet Press Ltd for *In a Country Museum* from **Selected Poems** by Patricia Beer, Connie Bensley for *May* from **Progress Report**, Peterloo Poets; Carcanet Press for *Gallop* from **Dreams of Power** by Alison Brackenbury; Carcanet Press for *The First*

Year No VIII and *The Sandy Yard* from **Collected Poems** by E.J. Scovell; Carcanet Press for *Overheard in County Sligo* from **Selected Poems** by Gillian Clarke; Gwendolyn Brooks for *Beverly Hills, Chicago* and *a Song in the Front Yard* from **Blacks** The David Company, Chicago; Faber & Faber Ltd for *Rondeau Redoublé* from **Making Cocoa for Kingsley Amis** by Wendy Cope; Wendy Cope for *Sisters*; Eunice de Souza for *Marriages are Made* from **Fix**, Newground (Bombay 1979); Anvil Press Poetry for *Comprehensive* from **Standing Female Nude** by Carol Ann Duffy, 1985; Anvil Press Poetry for *Warming Her Pearls* from **Selling Manhattan** by Carol Ann Duffy, 1987; Anvil Press Poetry for *The Buddha's Wife* from **Mrs Carmichael** by Ruth Silcock, 1987; Bloodaxe Books for *Malta* by Helen Dunmore from **The Raw Garden**; Roger Garfitt and Bloodaxe Books for *Evening* and *Wilson Ward* from Frances Horovitz's **Collected Poems**; Oxford University Press New Zealand for *Wellington Letter XV* from Lauris Emond's **Selected Poems**; Peterloo Poets for *Dear Mr Lee* from U.A. Fanthorpe's **A Watching Brief** (1987); Peterloo Poets for *A Stone's Throw* by Elma Mitchell from **People Etcetera: Poems New and Selected** (1987); Peterloo Poets for *Make Believe* from Gerda Mayer's **A Heartache of Grass** (1988); Martin Secker & Warburg for *A Quiet Wedding* and *The Way we Live* from Vicki Feaver's **Close Relatives**; Century Hutchinson for *Remembering Jean Rhys* from Elaine Feinstein's **Badlands**; Marilyn Hacker and Onlywomen Press for *Conversation in the Park* from **Love, Death and the Changing of the Seasons** (1987); Marilyn Hacker for *To Iva, Two and a Half* from **Taking Notice**, Knopf; Chatto & Windus for *Dewpond and Black Drainpipes* and *A Voice in the Garden* from Selima Hill's **Saying Hello at the Station**; Chatto & Windus for *The Last Day of March* and *A Woman of a Certain Age* from Carol Rumens' **Selected Poems**; Louise Hudson for *Men, Who Needs Them?* from **Four Ways**, Phoenix Press (1985); Edinburgh University Press for *The Choosing* from Liz Lochhead's **Dreaming Frankenstein and Collected Poems**; Edinburgh University Press for *Favourite Shade* from Liz Lochhead's **True Confessions**; David Higham Associates for *Friendship* from Elizabeth Jennings' **Collected Poems** (Macmillan); David Higham Associates for *The Conceiving* by Penelope Shuttle from **The Orchard Upstairs** (Oxford University Press 1980); David Higham Associates for *Mississippi Winter IV*, *Gray* and *The Diamonds on Liz's Bosom* from Alice Walker's **Horses Make a Landscape Beautiful** (The Women's Press); John Johnson Ltd for *There are More Accidents in the Home Than on the Road* from **Life and Turgid Times of A. Citizen** by Jenny Joseph in **The Thinking Heart** (Secker & Warburg 1978); John Johnson Ltd for *Warning* by Jenny Joseph from **Rose in the Afternoon** (Dent 1974); Sylvia Kantaris for *Love Letter* from **The Tenth Muse** (Peterloo 1983; repr. Menhir 1986); McClelland & Stewart Ltd for *Let Me Make This Perfectly Clear* by Geraldine MacEwan from **Afterwords**; Micere Githae Mugo for *Daughter of My People, Sing!* from **Daughter of My People, Sing**; Giant Steps Press (The Nanholme Centre, Shaw Wood Road, Todmorden, Lancs DL14 6OA) for *Dream Play* and *My Way* from Dorothy Nimmo's **Homewards**; Colin Smythe Ltd for *Edible Anecdote no 24* by Julie O'Callaghan from **Edible Anecdotes** (The Dolmen Press); Gabriela Pearse for *Sistahs* from **Black Women Talk**; A.M. Heath for *In the Men's Room(s)* by Marge Piercy from **Circles on the Water**; Olwyn Hughes for *Mirror* from Sylvia Plath's **Collected Poems** (Faber & Faber © Ted Hughes 1971 & 81); Kathleen Raine for *Christmas Children* from **Collected Poems**; W.W. Norton for *Translations* and *Phenomenology of Anger 9* from Adrienne Rich's **The Fact of a Doorframe**; Angus & Robertson Publishers for *Age to Youth* from Judith Wright's **Selected Poems: Five Senses**.

INTRODUCTION

Most people can't be bothered with poetry, least of all with contemporary poetry. At social gatherings, I am tempted to avoid mentioning that I have anything to do with it. The conversation goes something like this:

'What do you do?'
'I am a writer.'
'What do you write?'

Sometimes I say I am a journalist, which is true. If I also own up to the other thing I do, i.e. writing poems, my interlocutor either looks extremely suspicious or, more commonly, uncomfortable.

'It's terrible,' he or she will say. 'I'm afraid I haven't read any poetry for years.'

As often as not, the person turns out to be a great reader of novels, stories, biographies, travel books – anything but the dreaded verse. I am not inclined to believe that these people are incapable of responding to poetry. I think the problem is that they lack confidence in their ability to do so. Somehow they have become convinced that poetry is too difficult, too mysterious, not for them. They haven't had the good fortune to find out that reading poetry can help you live your life.

It is my hope that this book will enable you to find out that you can enjoy poetry and find it helpful. Perhaps you are already quite sure you like poetry. For you these pages may offer an introduction to some poets whose work you didn't know before. I compiled this anthology with a particular audience in mind, girls aged 13-16. However, now that it's done, I can see no reason at all why it shouldn't also be read by grown-up women, or by men and teenage boys. And I hope it will be.

The idea for the book first came up during a lunch

with Rosemary Stones, an expert on children's books and currently an editor at Collins. We had been discussing various ideas for books for young people, none of which fired me with enthusiasm. Then we began talking about *More To Life Than Mr Right*, a collection of stories by women writers, compiled by Rosemary. This is intended primarily for teenage girls. It occurred to us that I could do something similar, using poems by women about their own or other women's experience. This immediately struck me as an exciting project and it has continued to be exciting during the months I have been working on it.

Why just women poets? Shouldn't girls read poems by men as well? Yes, of course they should, and they won't have any difficulty in finding anthologies whose contributors are mostly male. Mixed anthologies, like mixed social gatherings, have their advantages and their drawbacks. There's something to be said for excluding men, now and again, in order to give women a chance to come into their own. All-female social occasions, though I don't always look forward to them, usually turn out to be more interesting than the average party and they seem to leave me feeling stronger. Compiling this book has had a similar effect. If it does half as much for its readers as it has done for me, I shall be happy.

I never doubted that I would be able to find enough good, suitable poems. The problem, as I expected, has been that there are far too many for a volume this size. At an early stage I regretfully decided there wouldn't be any room for translations – all these poems were originally written in English. Narrowing the field in this way still hasn't enabled me to put in everything I would have liked to include. There are some good women poets whose names you won't find here and there are others who are under-represented. When difficult choices had to be made, I tried to consider the young reader, rather than the acknowledged stature of the poet. Accessibility was one important criterion –anything

I couldn't understand on a careful first reading was put aside. The original plan was to make this a book of work by living writers. However, Rosemary agreed that we shouldn't exclude certain poets who had died prematurely. Sylvia Plath died in 1963, Frances Horovitz in 1983 – the two poems included here were among the last she wrote – and Gwendolyn MacEwen in 1987. If these three were still alive, they would be younger than several other contributors.

Most of the poets in the book are based in the UK, though some of these were born elsewhere – Fleur Adcock in New Zealand, Amryl Johnson in Trinidad, Gerda Mayer in Czechoslovakia, Grace Nichols in Guyana. There are also several overseas contributors. The Americans – Maya Angelou, Gwendolyn Brooks, Marilyn Hacker, Maxine Kumin, Marge Piercy, Adrienne Rich, May Swenson and Alice Walker – have all been published here, as well as in the USA. Sylvia Plath grew up in the USA but spent most of her adult life in England. Julie O'Callaghan also grew up in the States and now lives in Dublin. Gwendolyn MacEwen was Canadian, as is Margaret Atwood. Judith Wright is Australian, Lauris Edmond a New Zealander. Eunice de Souza is Indian.

The title *Is That The New Moon?* is from Elaine Feinstein's poem *Remembering Jean Rhys*. Jean Rhys, the novelist, died in 1979 at the age of 85. It seemed appropriate to take the title from a poem about a conversation between two women, the more so because Elaine's poem says something important about being a writer, and says it in a way that I find very moving.

The poems are arranged in alphabetical order according to titles. I owe this idea to Ted Hughes and Seamus Heaney, editors of *The Rattlebag* (Faber & Faber), where it works beautifully. I tried it out on these poems, liked some of the sequences it created, and left them like that.

Finally, if you are not used to reading poetry, don't feel

that you have to begin at the beginning of the volume and plod through to the end. Read whatever looks to you as if it might be interesting. Read slowly and, if you like the poem, read it again – you'll probably get more out of it the second time. Don't worry if you don't like everything. It's quite possible that nobody except me will like all these poems. If there is anything at all here that you want to go back to and read over and over again, then you have the capacity to respond to poetry. Keep looking, in this book and in others, for more poems you enjoy. The time won't be wasted.

Wendy Cope, August 1988

Judith Wright

AGE TO YOUTH

The sooty bush in the park
is green as any forest
for the boy to lie beneath,
with his arms around his dearest;

the black of the back street
is washed as any cloud
when the girl and the boy
touch hands among the crowd.

No, nothing's better than love,
than to want and to hold:
it is wise in the young
to forget the common world:

to be lost in the flesh
and the light shining there:
not to listen to the old
whose tune is fear and care—

who tell them love's a drink
poisoned with sorrow,
the flesh a flower today
and withered by tomorrow.

It is wise in the young
to let heart go racing heart,
to believe that the earth
is young and safe and sweet;

and the message we should send
from age back to youth
is that every kiss and glance
is truer than the truth;

that whatever we repent
of the time that we live,
it is never what we give—
it is never that we love.

BEAUTY

Beauty
is a fat black woman
walking the fields
pressing a breezed
hibiscus
to her cheek
while the sun lights up
her feet

Beauty
is a fat black woman
riding the waves
drifting in happy oblivion
while the sea turns back
to hug her shape

Carole Satyamurti

BETWEEN THE LINES

Words were dust-sheets, blinds.
People dying randomly, for 'want of breath',
shadowed my bed-times.
Babies happened;
adults buried questions under bushes.

Nouns would have been too robust
for body-parts; they were
curt, homeless prepositions—'inside',
'down there', 'behind', 'below'. No word
for what went on in darkness, overheard.

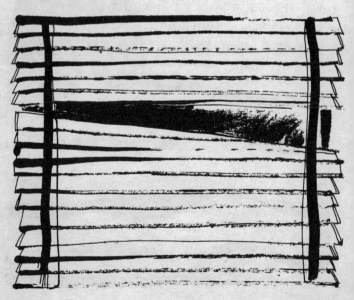

Underground, straining for language
that would let me out, I pressed to the radio,
read forbidden books. And once
visited Mr Cole. His seventeen
budgerigars praised God continually.

He loved all words, he said, though he used
few to force a kiss. All that summer
I longed to ask my mother, starved myself,
prayed, imagined skirts were getting tight,
hoped jumping down ten stairs would put it right.

My parents fought in other rooms,
their tight-lipped murmuring muffled
by flock wallpaper.
What was wrong, what they had to say
couldn't be shared with me.

He crossed the threshold in a wordless
slam of doors. 'Gone to live near work'
my mother said, before she tracked down
my diary, broke the lock, made me cut out
pages that guessed what silence was about.

Gwendolyn Brooks

BEVERLY HILLS, CHICAGO

"and the people live till they have white hair"
                                        —E.M. Price

The dry brown coughing beneath their feet,
(Only a while, for the handyman is on his way)
These people walk their golden gardens.
We say ourselves fortunate to be driving by
    today.

That we may look at them, in their gardens where
The summer ripeness rots. But not raggedly.
Even the leaves fall down in lovelier patterns here.
And the refuse, the refuse is a neat brilliancy.

When they flow sweetly into their houses
With softness and slowness touched by that
    everlasting gold,
We know what they go to. To tea. But that
    does not mean
They will throw some little black dots into
    some water and add sugar and the juice of
    the cheapest lemons that are sold,

While downstairs that woman's vague
  phonograph bleats, "Knock me a kiss."
And the living all to be made again in the
  sweatingest physical manner
Tomorrow . . . Not that anybody is saying that
  these people have no trouble.
Merely that it is trouble with a gold-flecked
  beautiful banner.

Nobody is saying that these people do not
     ultimately cease to be. And
Sometimes their passings are even more painful
     than ours.
It is just that so often they live till their hair
     is white.
They make excellent corpses, among the
     expensive flowers . . .

Nobody is furious. Nobody hates these people.
At least, nobody driving by in this car.
It is only natural, however, that it should occur
     to us
How much more fortunate they are than we are.

It is only natural that we should look and look
At their wood and brick and stone
And think, while a breath of pine blows,
How different these are from our own.

We do not want them to have less.
But it is only natural that we should think we
     have not enough.
We drive on, we drive on.
When we speak to each other our voices are
     a little gruff.

Ruth Silcock

THE BUDDHA'S WIFE

It can't have been fun for the Buddha's wife,
Left on her own for the rest of her life
When her good lord fled
The royal bed
To seek for his own perfection.

It's said in praise of Mahatma Gandhi –
A sort of saint, though his legs were bandy,
He was skinny and quaint – but still, a saint –
That for years he had nothing to do with his wife:
What about her life?

Christian women wear hats in church,
For fear lest their worshipping husbands lurch
And stagger and stare
At the sight of their hair,
Shining and heavy and long and free;
'Christian women shall not tempt me',
Said stern St. Paul, who refused to fall
Twice over, and made all women cover
Their burning and moving hair.

'Come,' said the milkmaids, 'come, come, come',
To their lord, Lord Krishna; who will not come.
The milkmaids dance and cry to the dawn,
White milk, white flowers on an emerald lawn,
The milkmaids call and the tired cows yawn
And nobody comes.

According to men, God has chosen men
To be his voice, his hand, his pen,
To utter his laws, to touch his grace,
To write his books, to read his face,
To be his channel to everyone human
Except a woman.

Liz Lochhead

THE CHOOSING

We were first equal Mary and I
with same coloured ribbons in mouse-coloured
    hair

and with equal shyness,
we curtseyed to the lady councillor
for copies of Collins' Children's Classics.
First equal, equally proud.

Best friends too Mary and I
a common bond in being cleverest
    (equal)
in our small school's small class.
I remember
the competition for top desk
at school service.
And my terrible fear
of her superiority at sums.

I remember the housing scheme
where we both stayed.
The same houses, different homes,
where the choices were made.

I don't know exactly why they moved,
but anyway they went.
Something about a three-apartment
and a cheaper rent.

But from the top deck of the
  high-school bus
I'd glimpse among the others on the
  corner
Mary's father, mufflered, contrasting
  strangely
with the elegant greyhounds by his side.
He didn't believe in high school
  education,
especially for girls,
or in forking out for uniforms.

Ten years later on a Saturday—
I am coming from the library—
sitting near me on the bus,
Mary
with a husband who is tall,
curly haired, has eyes
for no one else but Mary.
Her arms are round the full-shaped vase

that is her body.
Oh, you can see where the attraction lies
in Mary's life—
not that I envy her, really.

And I am coming from the library
with my arms full of books.
I think of those prizes that were ours for
  the taking
and wonder when the choices got made
we don't remember making.

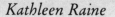

Kathleen Raine

CHRISTMAS CHILDREN

Little children running
Each in a paradise
Within, as Eden was,
Where invisible shine
London's many-coloured fairy-lights
Of Christmas-trees from far
Forests of night
Sheltering home, father, mother,
Puss, the koala-bears,
Tangerines, sugar-mice, a star.
Here and now boundless
Their merriment.

The dark hells walk past them unseen.

Sheenagh Pugh

COMING INTO THEIR OWN

I like to think of a day for all those
who have been unloved in legend; the crooked
   man
who married Morfudd, the mocked Menelaus,
Conchubhar, Mark of Cornwall, all whose pain

has been a good joke since the troubadours.
Always in the way, the comic hindrance
to the real hero; butts of tolerance.
Tristan had his day; it will come yours.

Stand up, sad, jealous, commonplace,
and make a flag out of the loneliness
you were supposed to suffer out of sight.
Embarrass us; make us admit to it.

Carol Ann Duffy

COMPREHENSIVE

Tutumantu is like hopscotch, Kwani-kwani is
    like hide-and-seek.
When my sister came back to Africa she could
    only speak
English. Sometimes we fought in bed because
    she didn't know
what I was saying. I like Africa better than
    England.
My mother says You will like it when we get
    our own house.
We talk a lot about the things we used to do
in Africa and then we are happy.

Wayne. Fourteen. Games are for kids. I support
the National Front. Paki-bashing and pulling
    girls'
knickers down. Dad's got his own mini-cab.
    We watch
the video. I Spit on Your Grave. Brilliant.
I don't suppose I'll get a job. It's all them
coming over here to work. Arsenal.

Masjid at 6 o'clock. School at 8. There was
a friendly shop selling flour. They kneaded
    it at home
to make the evening nan. Families face Mecca.

There was much more room to play than here
    in London.
We played in an old village. It is empty now.
We got a plane to Heathrow. People wrote to us
that everything was easy here.

It's boring. Get engaged. Probably work in
    Safeways
worst luck. I haven't lost it yet because I want
respect. Marlon Frederic's nice but he's a bit dark.
I like Madness. The lead singer's dead good.
My mum is bad with her nerves. She won't
let me do nothing. Michelle. It's just boring.

Ejaz. They put some sausages on my plate.
As I was going to put one in my mouth
a Moslem boy jumped on me and pulled.

The plate dropped on the floor and broke. He
    asked me in Urdu
if I was a Moslem. I said Yes. You shouldn't
    be eating this.
It's a pig's meat. So we became friends.

My sister went out with one. There was murder.
I'd like to be mates, but they're different from us.
Some of them wear turbans in class. You can't
    help
taking the piss. I'm going in the Army.
No choice really. When I get married
I might emigrate. A girl who can cook
with long legs. Australia sounds all right.

Some of my family are named after the Moghul
    emperors.
Aurangzeb, Jehangir, Babur, Humayun. I was
    born
thirteen years ago in Jhelum. This is a hard
    school.
A man came in with a milk crate. The teacher
    told us
to drink our milk. I didn't understand what
    she was saying,
so I didn't go to get any milk. I have hope
    and am ambitious.
At first I felt as if I was dreaming, but I wasn't.
Everything I saw was true.

Penelope Shuttle

THE CONCEIVING
(for Zoe)

Now
you are in the ark of my blood
in the river of my bones
in the woodland of my muscles
in the ligaments of my hair
in the wit of my hands
in the smear of my shadow
in the armada of my brain
under the stars of my skull
in the arms of my womb
Now you are here
you worker in the gold of flesh

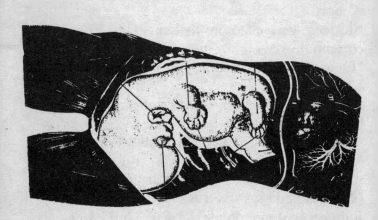

Marilyn Hacker

CONVERSATION IN THE PARK

"Do people look at me and know I'm gay?
It's not a problem you would have, because
only a girl goes down the stairs that way,

one at a time, and pigeon-toed. I'm splay-
footed, and I walk like a workhorse
—do people look at me and know I'm gay?"

"What you've got's *style*! Androgyny's passé
—you're all at once tough and voluptuous.
A girl only goes down the stairs that way
with two inside breast pockets, and the key
to a new BMW . . ." "Less prose!
Do people look at me and know I'm gay?"

"The uniform of the politically
correct, dear, would be grounds for a divorce!"
"Only—a girl gets down! The stares—that way

my back aches when I wonder what they say
behind it . . . But you wouldn't know. You
    chose!"
"Do people look at *me* and know I'm gay?"

"Honey, you look like a twelve-year-old boy.
But you go down on me the way, God knows,
only a girl goes down!" "The stairs! That way

out of the park, or else I'm going to lay
you right here, right now, on the grass!" "Yes,
  boss!
Do people look at us and know we're gay?"
"Why *would* two girls go down the stairs this
  way?"

Micere Githae Mugo

DAUGHTER OF MY PEOPLE, SING!

sing daughter sing
make a song
and sing
beat out your own rhythms
the rhythms of your life
but make the song soulful
and make life
sing

32

U.A. Fanthorpe

DEAR MR LEE

Dear Mr Lee (Mr Smart says
it's rude to call you Laurie, but that's
how I think of you, having lived with you
really all year), Dear Mr Lee
(Laurie) I just want you to know
I used to hate English, and Mr Smart
is roughly my least favourite person,
and as for Shakespeare (we're doing him too)
I think he's a national disaster, with all those jokes
that Mr Smart has to explain why they're jokes,
and even then no one thinks they're funny,
And T. Hughes and P. Larkin and that lot
in our anthology, not exactly a laugh a minute,
pretty gloomy really, so that's why
I wanted to say Dear Laurie (sorry) your book's
the one that made up for the others, if you
could see my copy you'd know it's lived
with me, stained with Coke and Kitkat
and when I had a cold, and I often
take you to bed with me to cheer me up
so Dear Laurie, I want to say sorry,
I didn't want to write a character-sketch
of your mother under headings, it seemed
wrong somehow when you'd made her so lovely,
and I didn't much like those questions
about *social welfare in the rural community*
and *the seasons as perceived by an adolescent*,

I didn't think you'd want your book
read that way, but bits of it I know by heart,
and I wish I had your uncles and your half-sisters
and lived in Slad, though Mr Smart says your view
of the class struggle is naïve, and the examiners
won't be impressed by me knowing so much
    by heart,
they'll be looking for terse and cogent answers
to their questions, but I'm not much good at
    terse and cogent,
I'd just like to be like you, not mind about
    being poor,
see everything bright and strange, the way
    you do,
and I've got the next one out of the Public
    Library,
about Spain, and I asked Mum about learning
to play the fiddle, but Mr Smart says Spain isn't
like that anymore, it's all Timeshare villas
and Torremolinos, and how old were you
when you became a poet? (Mr Smart says for
    anyone
with my punctuation to consider poetry as a
    career
is enough to make the angels weep).

PS   Dear Laurie, please don't feel guilty for
me failing the exam, it wasn't your fault,
it was mine, and Shakespeare's,
and maybe Mr Smart's, I still love *Cider*,
it hasn't made any difference.

Selima Hill

DEWPOND AND BLACK DRAIN-PIPES

In order to distract me, my mother
sent me on an Archaeology Week.
We lived in tents on the downs,
and walked over to the site
every morning. It was an old dewpond.

There was a boy there called Charlie.
He was the first boy I had really met.
I was too shy to go to the pub,
but I hung around the camp every night
waiting for him to come back.

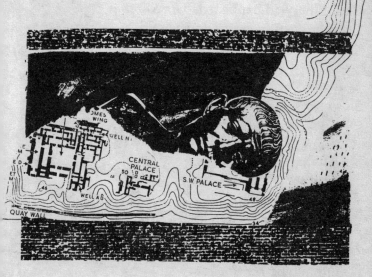

He took no notice of me at first,
but one night the two of us
were on Washing-Up together.
I was dressed in a black jersey
and black drain-pipes, I remember.

You in mourning? he said.
He didn't know I was
one of the first beatniks.
He put a drying-up cloth
over my head and kissed me

through the linen Breeds of Dogs.
I love you, Charlie I said.
Later, my mother blamed herself
for what had happened. *The Romans
didn't even interest her*, she said.

Alice Walker

THE DIAMONDS ON LIZ'S BOSOM

The diamonds on Liz's bosom
are not as bright
as his eyes
the morning they took him
to work in the mines
The rubies in Nancy's
jewel box (Oh, how he
loves red!)
not as vivid
as the despair
in his children's
frowns.

Oh, those Africans!

Everywhere you look
they're bleeding
and crying
Crying and bleeding
on some of the whitest necks
in your town.

Dorothy Nimmo

DREAM PLAY

I know there's something I must do today,
it's half an hour before curtain rise,
what is my part in this and what's the play?
there is a smell of greasepaint dust and size.

It's half an hour before curtain rise
this is the dressing room I know is mine,
there is a smell of greasepaint dust and size,
for God's sake tell me, what's the opening line?

This is the dressing room I know is mine
when they begin I'll recognise my cue.
For God's sake tell me, what's the opening line?
Who am I? What am I supposed to do?

When they begin I'll recognise my cue.
You're on! they whisper and I face the light.
Who am I? What am I supposed to do?
Forgive me, Mother. Have I got that right?

You're on! they whisper and I face the light
I say the line that they expect from me,
Forgive me Mother. Have I got that right?
Was it the daughter that I had to be?

I say the line that they expect from me
My voice is strangled. I'm awake. I shout
It was the daughter that I had to be
and I can't do it. You must write me out.

My voice is strangled. I'm awake. I shout
I know there's something I must do today
and I can't do it. You must write me out.
It's not my part and this is not my play.

Julie O'Callaghan

EDIBLE ANECDOTE No 24

the first thing you say is
'May I help you Ma'am?'
if she answers 'I'm still deciding'
well then you reply
'Our special for the day
is imported chocolate-covered cherries,
one dollar and ten cents a pound.
Would you care for a sample?'
She'll always say yes to that
even if she knows all she wants
is a pound and a half of chocolate raisins

don't watch them while they're sampling
except out of the corner of your eye
it makes them self-conscious
'My that *was* tasty' she'll sigh
as she wipes the syrup off her chin
'How much did you say those were?'
'One dollar and ten cents, Ma'am,
will I give you a pound or two?'
'Well, I *am* trying to watch my waistline,
but I will take a pound and a half
of chocolate raisins.'

then you say 'Why Ma'am, you certainly
don't look like you need to count your calories.'
as you're shovelling the raisins onto the scale
make sure she's looking and put a little extra in
that way when you say 'Will that be all?'
she may just giggle 'Oh, I'm in a naughty mood
    today,
you can give me a pound of those cherries as well'
say 'Yes Ma'am' humbly so she won't notice
you persuaded her.

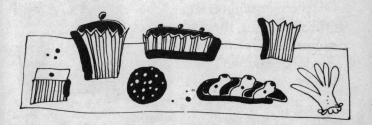

Frances Horovitz

EVENING

    Lilac blossom crests the window sill
mingling whiteness with the good dark of this
   room.
A bloom of light hangs delicately in white painted
   angles.
Bluebells heaped in a pot
still hold their blue against the dark;
I see their green stalks glisten.

    Thin as a swan's bone
I wait for the lessons of pain and light.
Grief is a burden, useless.
It must dissolve into the dark.
I see the hills, luminous.
There will be the holly tree
the hawthorn with mistletoe
foxgloves springing in thousands.

The hills also will pass away
        will remain
as this lilac light, these blue bells,
the good dark of this room.

Liz Lochhead

FAVOURITE SHADE
(Rap)

She's getting No More Black, her.
You've got bugger all bar black, Barbra.
Black's dead drab an' all.
Ah'd never have been seen
deid in it, your age tae!
Dreich. As a shade it's draining.
Better aff
somethin tae pit a bit a colour in her cheeks,
    eh no?

Black. Hale wardrobe fulla black claes.
Jist hingin' therr half the time, emmty.
On the hangers, hingin.
Plus by the way a gloryhole
Chockablock with bermuda shorts, the lot.
Yella Kimono, ah don't know
whit all.
Tropical prints.
Polyester everything Easy-Kerr. Bit naw, naw
that was last year, noo
she's no one to give
nothing coloured
houseroom. Black. Black.
Ah'm fed up tae the back teeth lukkin' ett her.
Feyther says the same.

Who's peyin' fur it onlywey?
Wance yir workin' weer whit yi like.
No as if yiv nothin' tae pit oan yir back.
Black!
As well oot the world as oot the fashion.

Seen a wee skirt in Miss Selfridge.
Sort of dove, it was lovely.
Would she weer it, but?
Goes: see if it was black
it'd be brilliant.

E.J. Scovell

THE FIRST YEAR NO VIII

The baby in her blue night-jacket, propped on
   hands
With head raised, coming out to day, has
   half-way sloughed
The bed-clothes, as a sea-lion, as a mermaid
Half sloughs the sea, rooted in sea, basking on
   strands.

Like a gentle coastal creature she looks round
At one who comes and goes the far side of
   her bars;
Firm in her place and lapped by blankets; here
   like tides
Familiar rise and fall our care for her, our sounds.

Elizabeth Jennings

FRIENDSHIP

Such love I cannot analyse;
It does not rest in lips or eyes,
Neither in kisses nor caress.
Partly, I know, it's gentleness

And understanding in one word
Or in brief letters. It's preserved
By trust and by respect and awe.
These are the words I'm feeling for.

Two people, yes, two lasting friends.
The giving comes, the taking ends.
There is no measure for such things.
For this all Nature slows and sings.

Alison Brackenbury

GALLOP

An unholy conspiracy
of girls and horses, I admit,
as never being part in it
but riding late and anxiously.
On Sunday when the horses climb the hill
scrambling the dried watercourse to reach
the open field to gallop: all my breath
swells hot inside me as the horses bunch
and pull for mad speed, even my old horse—

'gently!' the leader calls—but they are gone,
hunters, young horses, surging hard ahead,
I rocked across the saddle, the wet soil
flung shining past me, and the raking feet
shaking me from stirrups as I speak
breathless, kind names to the tossing neck
haul back the reins, watching the widening gap
between my foundered horse and the fast pack,

wondering if I can keep on, why I do this;
and he falters, my legs tired as his,
I faintly understand this rage for speed:
careless and hard, what do they see ahead,
galloping down spring's white light, but a gate
a neat house, a small lawn, a cage of sunlight?

And pounding, slow, behind, I wish that I
rode surely as they do but wish I could
tell them what I see in sudden space—
Two flashing magpies rising from the trees
two birds: good omen; how the massive cloud
gleams and shadows over as they wait,
the horses blown and steaming at shut gates:
disclosing, past their bright heads, my dark wood.

Alison Fell

GIRL'S GIFTS

The soft whorls of my fingertips
against snapdragons:
I am making a flower basket for my grandmother.
A rose petal folds back, squares, curls under
One, two, many rose petals curl back
between my fingers
I search for the core which hides.
My grandmother is gentle today,
old. Bees hum over her.
Today she sits reading, not gardening,
not scolding.
The blossom on its branch holds juice which
a touch spills
I glance across the grass,
a shadow in the window is my mother
cooking, watching.
I am making a tiny secret basket for my
    grandmother.
My mouth waters
I would lick the green leaf, taste the bronze
and yellow silk of my snapdragon,
I mould petals, weave stems, with love
my little finger inches in the folds:
it is done, red and gold.
I will carry it cupped like a jewel or a robin's egg
It will lie, perfect, in her wrinkled palm
I will cross the grass and give it.

Carole Satyamurti

GIRLS' TALK

Then Miss Rodway sent the boys
out to the playground, and she told us
about the German measles injection
so we won't have deformed babies.

She said we could ask her
anything we liked. She twisted the ring
on her finger round and round,
swinging her legs.

I asked if there's a wrong way
to have sex; if the sperms always
find the way, or if they sometimes
get lost, spill on to the sheets.

The boys were jumping up outside the window;
Miss made cross shooing faces.
She said men have stronger urges,
that's why many marriages don't last.

Natalie's got periods already
even though she plays football.
Mr Davis won't let her go to the toilet
when she asks, because she's naughty.

She told us about the pill
but I wasn't listening—I was thinking
of what I do in bed at night
when bad dreams come out of the cupboard.

It wasn't the same as when you told me
—it seemed so serious
Catherine and I couldn't stop laughing;
we stuffed tissues in our mouths.

But Mum, I'm scared of the injection.

Elizabeth Bartlett

GOD IS DEAD–NIETZSCHE

Daddy and I are always here, you know,
Whenever you want us.
We didn't like the things you said
The last time home.
Bourgeois, you said, and a word which sounded
Very like atrophied.
Daddy doesn't like the way you collect
Toilet graffiti,
God is dead—Nietzsche, and the reply,
Nietzsche is dead—God.

You can't expect Daddy to go round
With the plate in church
With thoughts like that in his head.
I worry too.
Structuralism sounds like a building-site,
Semiology sounds rather rude
In a medical kind of way.
The dogs are well, both almost human,
As we've often said
To you.

Please wear a vest, the days are getting
Colder. We hope you will not be so rude
The next time home.
Daddy and I have just re-done your room.
The blood on the wall hardly shows
After two coats of paint.
Cambridge must be very pretty just now.
I am, in spite of everything,
Your loving Mother.

Alice Walker

GRAY

I have a friend
who is turning gray,
not just her hair,
and I do not know
why this is so.

Is it a lack of vitamin E
pantothenic acid, or B-12?
Or is it from being frantic
and alone?

"How long does it take you to love someone?"
I ask her.
"A hot second," she replies.
"And how long do you love them?"
"Oh, anywhere up to several months."
"And how long does it take you
to get over loving them?"
"Three weeks," she said, "tops."

Did I mention I am also
turning gray?
It is because I *adore* this woman
who thinks of love
in this way.

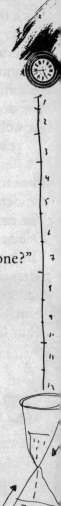

Patricia Beer

IN A COUNTRY MUSEUM

This is a strange museum. In one square yard see
A mummified ibis and a postilion's boot.
Grey litter fills the house. For years every dead
    man
Had some cast-off curious object to donate.

Mindless and slovenly it is, but in one room,
Close to five jars that once held Daffy's Elixir,
Lies something that takes shape. A pallid
    patchwork quilt
Wrapped in cellophane, is spread on a
    four-poster.

A card describes the maker, a fourteen-year-old
Servant girl, with no book-learning and no
    siblings,
Who saved up half-a-crown for the big central
    piece
Of cloth, and got up at dawn on summer
    mornings.

This sounds sober and worthy, but the card
    goes on
To say that, interviewed at eighty, Mrs Brew
Declared it had given her much greater pleasure
Than anything in all her life. If it is true

That to labour on these plodding squares meant
    more
Than marriage bed, children and a belief in God,
It is the best country marvel in this building
And suitably placed among these bright fields
    of food.

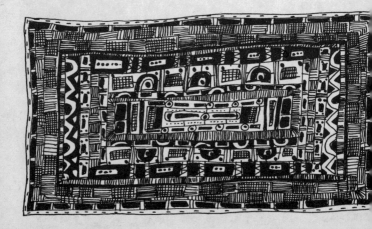

Anne Stevenson

INCIDENT

She must have been about
twelve in 1942.

She stood in front
of the tall hall mirror
and she made a mou.
With her pretty not-
yet-kissed mouth she made an ugly
mou mou
that didn't mean anything she
knew.
So bony, so skinny
and so very naked.
Little pink belled breasts like dew.

The mirror did what she did –
mou mou   mou mou

Nowhere to go.
Nothing to do.

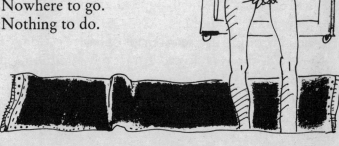

Marge Piercy

IN THE MEN'S ROOM(S)

When I was young I believed in intellectual
    conversation:
I thought the patterns we wove on stale smoke
floated off to the heaven of ideas.
To be certified worthy of high masculine
    discourse
like a potato on a grater I would rub on contempt,
suck snubs, wade proudly through the brown
    stuff on the floor.
They were talking of integrity and existential
    ennui
while the women ran out for six-packs and had
    abortions
in the kitchen and fed the children and were
    auctioned off.

Eventually of course I learned how their eyes
    perceived me:
when I bore to them cupped in my hands a
    new poem to nibble,
when I brought my aerial maps of Sartre or Marx,
they said, she is trying to attract our attention,
she is offering up her breasts and thighs.
I walked on eggs, their tremulous equal:
they saw a fish peddler hawking in the street.

Now I get coarse when the abstract nouns start
    flashing.
I go out to the kitchen to talk cabbages and habits.
I try hard to remember to watch what people do.
Yes, keep your eyes on the hands, let the voice
    go buzzing.
Economy is the bone, politics is the flesh,
watch who they beat and who they eat,
watch who they relieve themselves on, watch
    who they own.
The rest is decoration.

May Swenson

THE JAMES BOND MOVIE

The popcorn is greasy, and I forgot to bring
    a Kleenex.
A pill that's a bomb inside the stomach of a
    man inside

The Embassy blows up. Eructations of flame,
    luxurious
cauliflowers giganticize into motion. The entire
    29-ft.

screen is orange, is crackling flesh and brick
    bursting,
blackening, smithereened. I unwrap a Dentyne
    and, while

jouncing my teeth in rubber tongue-smarting
    clove, try
with the 2-inch-wide paper to blot butter off
    my fingers.

A bubble-bath, room-sized, in which 14 girls,
    delectable
and sexless, twist-topped Creamy Freezes (their
    blond,

red, brown, pinkish, lavender or silver wiglets all
screwed that high, and varnished), scrub-tickle
    a lone

male, whose chest has just the right amount
    and distribu-
tion of curly hair. He's nervously pretending
    to defend

his modesty. His crotch, below the waterline,
    is also
below the frame—but unsubmerged all 28 slick
    foamy boobs.

Their makeup fails to let the girls look naked.
    Caterpil-
lar lashes, black and thick, lush lips glossed pink
    like

the gum I pop and chew, contact lenses on the
    eyes that are
mostly blue, they're nose-perfect replicas of each
    other.

I've got most of the grease off and onto this
    little square
of paper. I'm folding it now, making creases
    with my nails.

Fleur Adcock

KISSING

The young are walking on the riverbank,
arms around each other's waists and shoulders,
pretending to be looking at the waterlilies
and what might be a nest of some kind, over
there, which two who are clamped together
mouth to mouth have forgotten about.
The others, making courteous detours
around them, talk, stop talking, kiss.
They can see no one older than themselves.
It's their river. They've got all day.

Seeing's not everything. At this very
moment the middle-aged are kissing
in the backs of taxis, on the way
to airports and stations. Their mouths and
    tongues
are soft and powerful and as moist as ever.
Their hands are not inside each other's clothes
(because of the driver) but locked so tightly
together that it hurts: it may leave marks
on their not of course youthful skin, which they
    won't
notice. They too may have futures.

Carol Rumens

THE LAST DAY OF MARCH

The elms are darkened by rain.
On the small, park-sized hills
Sigh the ruined daffodils
As if they shared my refrain
– That when I leave here, I lose
All reason to see you again.

What's finishing was so small,
I never mentioned it.
My time, like yours, was full,
And I would have blushed to admit
How shallow the rest could seem;
How so little could be all.

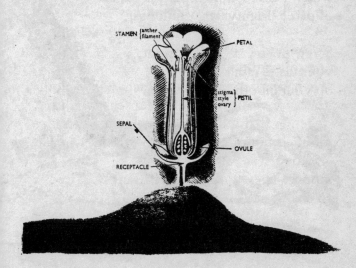

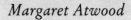

Margaret Atwood

LATE NIGHT

Late night and rain wakes me, a downpour,
wind thrashing in the leaves, huge
ears, huge feathers,
like some chased animal, a giant
dog or wild boar. Thunder & shivering
windows; from the tin roof
the rush of water.

I lie askew under the net,
tangled in damp cloth, salt in my hair.
When this clears there will be fireflies
& stars, brighter than anywhere,
which I could contemplate at times
of panic. Lightyears, think of it.

Screw poetry, it's you I want,
your taste, rain
on you, mouth on your skin.

Gwendolyn MacEwen

LET ME MAKE THIS PERFECTLY CLEAR

Let me make this perfectly clear.
I have never written anything because it is a
    Poem.
This is a mistake you always make about me,
A dangerous mistake. I promise you
I am not writing this because it is a Poem.

You suspect this is a posture or an act.
I am sorry to tell you it is not an act.

You actually think I care if this
Poem gets off the ground or not. Well
I don't care if this poem gets off the ground or not
And neither should you.
All I have ever cared about
And all you should ever care about
Is what happens when you lift your eyes from
    this page.

Do not think for one minute it is the Poem
    that matters.
It is not the Poem that matters.
You can shove the Poem.
What matters is what is out there in the large dark
And in the long light,
Breathing.

Grace Nichols

LIKE A FLAME

Raising up
from my weeding
of ripening cane

my eyes
make four
with this man

there ain't
no reason
to laugh

but
I laughing
in confusion

his hands
soft his words
quick his lips
curling as in
prayer

I nod

I like this man

Tonight
I go to meet him
like a flame

Sylvia Kantaris

LOVE-LETTER

There must be others in the house,
stuffed in old bags, old shoes,
old books especially.
This one turned up in a copy of
'Dr. Spock' and 'I shall love you always'
stares me in the face along with longings
as bottomless as oceans.
(We were moving over one in a big ship
in separate cabins.)
Consider the ingredients for romance—
one handsome male, unmarried,
one female, still in transit, who
could stand as wistfully as any
nineteenth-century heroine at the rail
with mandatory wind in flowing hair,
one baby in her arms (a little out of place here)
then, under the door in the early
hours, this hot and urgent letter . . .
They might have lived together ever after,
but on the envelope my scribbled list of needs
    reads:
'Farex, orange-juice, disposable nappies' and
'HELP!' in capitals. (The child
had had his way with me the whole long
feverish night.)
I'm sure I would have loved you
but the timing wasn't right.

Gerda Mayer

MAKE BELIEVE

Say I were not sixty,
say you weren't near-hundred,
say you were alive.
Say my verse was read
in some distant country,
and say you were idly turning the pages:

The blood washed from your shirt,
the tears from your eyes,
the earth from your bones;
neither missing since 1940,
nor dead as reported later
by a friend of a friend of a friend . . .

Quite dapper you stand in that bookshop
and chance upon my clues.

That is why at sixty
when some publisher asks me
for biographical details,
I still carefully give
the year of my birth,
the name of my hometown:

GERDA MAYER born '27, in Karlsbad,
Czechoslovakia . . . write to me, father.

NOTE: The author's father, Arnold Stein, escaped from the German concentration
camp in Nisko in 1939, fled to Russian-occupied Lemberg/Lwow, and then
disappeared in the summer of 1940. It is thought he may have died in a Russian
camp.

Helen Dunmore

MALTA

The sea's a featureless blaze.
On photographs nothing comes out
but glare, with that scarlet-rimmed fishing boat
far-off, lost to the lens.

At noon a stiff-legged tourist in shorts
steps, camera poised. He's stilted
as a flamingo, pink-limbed.

Icons of Malta gather around him.
He sweats as a procession passes
and women with church-dark faces
brush him as if he were air.

He holds a white crocheted dress
to give to his twelve-year-old daughter
who moons in the apartment, sun-sore.
The sky's tight as a drum, hard
to breathe in, hard to walk under.

He would not buy 'bikini for daughter'
though the man pressed him, with plump fingers
spreading out scraps of blue cotton.

Let her stay young, let her know nothing.
Let her body remain skimpy and sudden.
His wife builds arches of silence over her

new breasts and packets of tampons marked
    'slender'.
At nights, when they think she's asleep,
they ache in the same places
but never louder than a whisper.

He watches more women melt into a porch.
Their white, still laundry flags from window
    to window
while they are absent, their balconies blank.

At six o'clock, when he comes home and snicks
his key in the lock so softly neither will catch it
he hears one of them laugh.
They are secret in the kitchen, talking of nothing,
strangers whom anyone might love.

Eunice De Souza

MARRIAGES ARE MADE

My cousin Elena
is to be married.
The formalities
have been completed:
her family history examined
for T.B. and madness
her father declared solvent
her eyes examined for squints
her teeth for cavities
her stools for the possible
non-Brahmin worm.
She's not quite tall enough
and not quite full enough
(children will take care of that)
Her complexion it was decided
would compensate, being just about
the right shade
of rightness
to do justice to
Francisco X. Noronha Prabhu
good son of Mother Church.

fit for ▩ X

Connie Bensley

MAY

They're cutting grass below in Lincoln's Inn,
And by her desk, soft air is drifting in
With hints of lilac. Seven hours to go
Between these walls. 'Dear Sir', the hours begin.

'Dear Sir, . . . My dearest Sir' her fingers say
(With carbon copies) 'write to me today,
And tell me what you look like, who you are,
And if you feel the summer on its way'.

Louise Hudson

MEN, WHO NEEDS THEM?

Now I go to films alone
watch a silent telephone
send myself a valentine
whisper softly 'I am mine'

Sylvia Plath

MIRROR

I am silver and exact. I have no preconceptions.
Whatever I see I swallow immediately
Just as it is, unmisted by love or dislike.
I am not cruel, only truthful—
The eye of a little god, four-cornered.
Most of the time I meditate on the opposite wall.
It is pink, with speckles. I have looked at it
    so long
I think it is a part of my heart. But it flickers.
Faces and darkness separate us over and over.

Now I am a lake. A woman bends over me,
Searching my reaches for what she really is.
Then she turns to those liars, the candles or
    the moon.
I see her back, and reflect it faithfully.
She rewards me with tears and an agitation of
    hands.
I am important to her. She comes and goes.
Each morning it is her face that replaces the
    darkness.
In me she has drowned a young girl, and in
    me an old woman
Rises toward her day after day, like a terrible fish.

Alice Walker

MISSISSIPPI WINTER IV

My father and mother both
used to warn me
that "a whistling woman and a crowing
hen would surely come to
no good end." And perhaps I should
have listened to them.
But even at the time I knew
that though my end probably might
not
be good
I must whistle
like a woman undaunted
until I reached it.

Dorothy Nimmo

MY WAY

I know the difference between right and wrong
I learnt about it at my mother's knee
and all the good belonged of right to her
and all the bad I knew was left to me.

Hers the white innocence behind the veil,
the calm blue passage on the roughest sea
the rose-pink silence and the golden hymn
and hers the comfort of forgiving me.

Mine the red glow of anger, steely tongued,
boredom, green jealousy and black despair,
hatred and envy, pale dreams, purple rage,
the wicked pain of not forgiving her.

I went my way. I knew my way was wrong
and so I feel it every blasted day.
She didn't give me any other choice.
I couldn't leave her any other way.

Dorothy Byrne

NICE MEN

I know a nice man who is kind to his wife
and always lets her do what she wants.

I heard of another nice man who killed his
girlfriend. It was an accident. He pushed her
in a quarrel and she split open her skull on the
dining-room table. He was such a guilt-ridden
sight in court that the jury felt sorry for him.

My friend Aiden is nice. He thinks women are
really equal.

There are lots of nice men who help their wives
with the shopping and the housework.

And many men, when you are alone with
them, say, 'I prefer women. They are so
understanding.' This is another example of
men being nice.

Some men, when you make a mistake at work,
just laugh. They don't go on about it or shout.
That's nice.

At times, the most surprising men will say at
parties, 'There's a lot to this Women's Lib.'
Here again, is a case of men behaving in a nice
way.

Another nice thing is that some men are
    sympathetic when their wives feel unhappy.
I've often heard men say, 'Don't worry about
    everything so much, dear.'

You hear stories of men who are far more than
    nice – putting women in lifeboats first, etc.

Sometimes when a man has not been nice, he
    apologises and trusts you with intimate details
    of the pressures in his life. This just shows how
    nice he is, underneath.

I think that is all I can say on the subject of
    nice men. Thank you.

Gillian Clarke

OVERHEARD IN COUNTY SLIGO

I married a man from County Roscommon
and I live at the back of beyond
with a field of cows and a yard of hens
and six white geese on the pond.

At my door's a square of yellow corn
caught up by its corners and shaken,
and the road runs down through the open gate
and freedom's there for the taking.

I had thought to work on the Abbey stage
or have my name in a book,
to see my thought on the printed page,
or still the crowd with a look.

But I turn to fold the breakfast cloth
and to polish the lustre and brass,
to order and dust the tumbled rooms
and find my face in the glass.

I ought to feel I'm a happy woman
for I lie in the lap of the land,
and I married a man from County Roscommon
and I live in the back of beyond.

Maxine Kumin

PARTING

Each year in the after-Christmas tinsel
of the airport lounge you see them
standing like toys that have been
wound up once or twice and then
shunted aside. Mother, father,
whose bodies time has thickened
to pudding, resolute daughter,
stylish and frightened.
That small a constellation,
that commonplace a grouping.

They are done with speaking.
They do not weep.
They do not touch one another except
after the final boarding call
when they are fastened all
three as in a dangerous struggle
exploding only as she
is drawn into the silver belly of the jet
and shot from the parents
and this is the celestial arrangement.

Pam Ayres

PAUL O'CHATBERG GROGAN

He was Paul O'Chatberg Grogan,
He was manly, he was lean,
The sun had bleached his hair
And it was thick and it was clean.
His eyes were cold as chisels
Far too blue for any man
And when he gazed on women
Well, they clutched their drawers and ran.

He was Paul O'Chatberg Grogan
Of the long athletic stride
With long athletic arms
All down his long athletic side,
With long athletic legs;
And those that knew the family well
Said he had a long athletic
History as well.

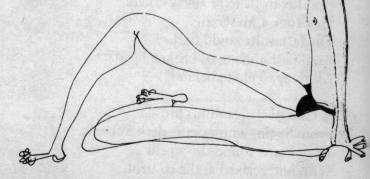

He was Paul O'Chatberg Grogan
He could ride and he could hunt
And when he was at Cambridge
He was mustard with a punt.
He could speak in any language
The world had ever known,
And when he got fed up with that
He wrote one of his own.

He was a demon on the squash court
And a tyrant in the gym;
He had a spotted belt in judo
(They'd invented it for him).
And when he hit a cricket ball
The sound was like no other's
For the bat disintegrated
And he had to use his brother's.

Oh, his gaze was always level,
His chin was always square,
His voice was always even
And his teeth were always there.
He drove a Maserati
The fastest he could find
And a little string of broken hearts
All flopped along behind.

A Countess shared his life –
From Spain, with eyes as dark as coals.
They jetted round the world
With him relaxed at the controls.

And she had hair like ebony
And she had skin like gold
With hands that felt like butterflies
And feet that felt the cold.

And she had feather pillows
And she had satin sheets,
And Paul O'Chatberg Grogan
Could perform amazing feats.
The feats he could perform
Cannot be decently revealed
But a chicken house collapsed
A mile behind them in a field.

Here lies Paul O'Chatberg Grogan
Place no headstone, lay no wreath.
One morning in the mirror
He was dazzled by his teeth.
The lonely Maserati
Is silent on the grass
And broken hearts jump up
And dash themselves against the glass.

Amryl Johnson

PEANUT VENDOR

Nuts! Nuts!
Frrrr-esh peanuts!
Reach fer yuh money!
Be quick! Be hasty!

Lady lookin' so pretty in de green dress
Stop, take a peep and see fer yuhself
Ah promise ah sellin' only de bes'

Nuts! Salted nuts!
Fresh an' crisp!
Put dem to yuh lips!
Dey better dan a kiss!

Girl, ah tell yuh dese nuts hot from de fire
Ah does roas' dem meself wit' love an' desire
Is de trut' Yuh tink ah is some kinda liar?

Nuts! Nuts!
Get yuh roasted nuts!
Good an' fresh!
Hot's de best!

Dou-dou yuh know yuh lookin' real nice
Earrings, shoes an' yuh hanbag jus' right
Tell meh, nah. Yuh wan' come home tonight?

Fresh nuts!
Roas' today!
So warm dey go burn yuh clothes!
So fresh dey sweeter dan any rose!

Darlin' ah love yuh as soon as ah see yuh
Ah hah a car, meh own house an' a lotta property
Leave yuh husban', ah sure ah go make yuh
    real happy

Stop fer yuh nuts!
Dohn be in a rush!
Ah sellin' out fas'!
Meh stock wohn las'!

Ah eh know wha' wrong wit' all yuh women
Ah talkin' nice an' ting an' yuh still eh answerin'
An' worse dan dat, it look like yuh eh wan'
    buy meh

Nuts! Nuts!
Salted nuts!
Fresh an' tasty!
Be quick! Be hasty!

Adrienne Rich

THE PHENOMENOLOGY OF ANGER No 9

The only real love I have ever felt
was for children and other women.
Everything else was lust, pity,
self-hatred, pity, lust.
This is a woman's confession.
Now, look again at the face
of Botticelli's Venus, Kali,
the Judith of Chartres
with her so-called smile.

Vicki Feaver

A QUIET WEDDING

They have no photographs –
not even hidden
in a drawer.

But they'll have to tell
the children something
when they ask

and after all this time
it should be safe
to look back.

The day's still there –
not as they'd imagined
softened to a blur

but dark and hard
like the discarded drink
she found long after

dried up in a glass:
his cough echoing
in the almost empty church,

faces stiffened into smiles,
someone's tactless joke
about a pram (his sister crying),

waving goodbye from a train,
and later, in a hotel room
that smelt of cigarettes and beer,

turning back used sheets,
thinking it's all over
and only just beginning.

Elaine Feinstein

REMEMBERING JEAN RHYS

– Is that the new moon, that
   fine white line on the night, look,
through the hotel window? Then she covered up
   enormous eyes, to hide the dangerous sign.
And some cowardice made me lie.

Too much ill-luck had already happened,
   I suppose. Now, in her seventies, however late,
I wanted her to be having a fling and a treat
   unworried by some message from the skies
she might believe.

She listened for a moment like a child,
   smiling, and yet I saw
under the blue credulity of her gaze
   a writer's spirit,
and that was not deceived.

Wendy Cope

RONDEAU REDOUBLÉ

There are so many kinds of awful men –
One can't avoid them all. She often said
She'd never make the same mistake again:
She always made a new mistake instead.

The chinless type who made her feel ill-bred;
The practised charmer, less than charming when
He talked about the wife and kids and fled –
There are so many kinds of awful men.

The half-crazed hippy, deeply into Zen,
Whose cryptic homilies she came to dread;
The fervent youth who worshipped Tony Benn –
'One can't avoid them all,' she often said.

The ageing banker, rich and overfed,
Who held forth on the dollar and the yen –
Though there were many more mistakes ahead,
She'd never make the same mistake again.

The budding poet, scribbling in his den
Odes not to her but to his pussy, Fred;
The drunk who fell asleep at nine or ten –
She always made a new mistake instead.

And so the gambler was at least unwed
And didn't preach or sneer or wield a pen
Or hoard his wealth or take the Scotch to bed.
She'd lived and learned and lived and learned
    but then
There are so many kinds.

E.J. Scovell

THE SANDY YARD

One day at noon I crossed
A sandy yard planted with citrus trees
Behind a small hotel. I walked slowly in the sun
With feet in the hot sand which the leaf-cutting
   ants
Crossed too, under their little sails of green, filing
Intent; and I thought, this
I will keep, I will register with time: I am here;
And always, shall have been here – that is the
   wonder –
Never, now, not have been here; for now I
   am here,
Crossing the sandy yard
Between the citrus trees, behind the small hotel.

Gabriela Pearse

SISTAHS

. . . And four five six
different coloured black
women gathered together
to share
our treasures.
We sat a ring
we put food in the middle
we started around.

Each gave
we were there—
not in our shyness
not in our histories
not in keeping any games up
Each gave
her utter presence that
rare bird that alights
once in a black full dark blood moon.

Each gave
complete hearing—
we heard so hard
we were in danger of becoming one.
Letting each other in
was exciting
we were excited

and bubbling
—connected.

We talked black-woman-talk
all the different sides of it
We were so loud
we laughed
    slapped thighs
    hooted and chortled
into the night.

We spoke the words
our mothers divided
    insane
    drunk and
    silenced
could not speak,
—boy we had centuries of
catchin' up to do.

Letting us share their pain
    and questions upon questions
    never asked—
they were watching us
sitting right behind us
slightly bewildered—
a bit shocked . . .
but smiling in their hearts.

Wendy Cope

SISTERS
(for Marian)

My sister
was the bad one –
said what she thought
and did what she liked
and didn't care.

At ten she wore
a knife tucked in
her leather belt,
dreamed of *being*
a prince on a white horse.

Became a dolly bird
with dyed hair longer
than her skirts, pulling
the best of the local talent.
Mother wept and prayed.

At thirty she's divorced,
has cropped her locks
and squats in Hackney –
tells me 'God created man
then realised Her mistake.'

I'm not like her,
I'm good – but now
I'm working on it.
Fighting through
to my own brand of badness

I am glad of her
at last – her conferences,
her anger, and her boots.
We talk and smoke
and laugh at everybody –

two bad sisters.

Gwendolyn Brooks

A SONG IN THE FRONT YARD

I've stayed in the front yard all my life.
I want a peek at the back
Where it's rough and untended and hungry weed
   grows.
A girl gets sick of a rose.

I want to go in the back yard now
And maybe down the alley,
To where the charity children play.
I want a good time today.

They do some wonderful things.
They have some wonderful fun.
My mother sneers, but I say it's fine
How they don't have to go in at quarter to nine.
My mother, she tells me that Johnnie Mae
Will grow up to be a bad woman.
That George'll be taken to Jail soon or late
(On account of last winter he sold our back gate).

But I say it's fine. Honest, I do.
And I'd like to be a bad woman, too,
And wear the brave stockings of night-black lace
And strut down the streets with paint on my face.

Maya Angelou

STILL I RISE

You may write me down in history
With your bitter, twisted lies,
You may trod me in the very dirt
But still, like dust, I'll rise.

Does my sassiness upset you?
Why are you beset with gloom?
'Cause I walk like I've got oil wells
Pumping in my living room.

Just like moons and like suns,
With the certainty of tides,
Just like hopes springing high,
Still I'll rise.

Did you want to see me broken?
Bowed head and lowered eyes?
Shoulders falling down like teardrops,
Weakened by my soulful cries.

Does my haughtiness offend you?
Don't you take it awful hard
'Cause I laugh like I've got gold mines
Diggin' in my own back yard.

You may shoot me with your words,
You may cut me with your eyes,
You may kill me with your hatefulness,
But still, like air, I'll rise.

Does my sexiness upset you?
Does it come as a surprise
That I dance like I've got diamonds
At the meeting of my thighs?

Out of the huts of history's shame
I rise
Up from a past that's rooted in pain
I rise
I'm a black ocean, leaping and wide,
Welling and swelling I bear in the tide.

Leaving behind nights of terror and fear
I rise
Into a daybreak that's wondrously clear
I rise
Bringing the gifts that my ancestors gave,
I am the dream and the hope of the slave.
I rise
I rise
I rise.

Elma Mitchell

A STONE'S THROW

We shouted out
'We've got her! Here she is!
It's her all right'.
We caught her.
There she was—

A decent-looking woman, you'd have said,
(They often are)
Beautiful, but dead scared,
Tousled—we roughed her up
A little, nothing much

And not the first time
By any means
She'd felt men's hands
Greedy over her body—
But ours were virtuous,
Of course.

And if our fingers bruised
Her shuddering skin,
These were love-bites, compared
To the hail of kisses of stone,
The last assault
And battery, frigid rape,
To come
Of right.

For justice must be done
Specially when
It tastes so good.

And then—this guru,
Preacher, God-merchant, God-knows-what-
Spoilt the whole thing,
Speaking to her
(Should never speak to them)
Squatting on the ground—her level,
Writing in the dust
Something we couldn't read.

And saw in her
Something we couldn't see,
At least until
He turned his eyes on us,
Her eyes on us,
Our eyes upon ourselves.

We walked away
Still holding stones
That we may throw
Another day
Given the urge.

St. John's Gospel, ch. 8, V. 3–11

Rosemary Tonks

STORY OF A HOTEL ROOM

Thinking we were safe—insanity!
We went in to make love. All the same
Idiots to trust the little hotel bedroom.
Then in the gloom . . .
. . . And who does not know that pair of shutters
With the awkward hook on them
All screeching whispers? Very well then, in the
    gloom
We set about acquiring one another
Urgently! But on a temporary basis
Only as guests—just guests of one another's
    senses.

But idiots to feel so safe you hold back nothing
Because the bed of cold, electric linen
Happens to be illicit . . .
To make love as well as that is ruinous.
Londoner, Parisian, someone should have
    warned us
That without permanent intentions
You have absolutely no protection
—If the act is clean, authentic, sumptuous,
The concurring deep love of the heart
Follows the naked work, profoundly moved by
    it.

Fleur Adcock

STREET SONG

Pink Lane, Strawberry Lane, Pudding Chare:
someone is waiting, I don't know where;
hiding among the nursery names,
he wants to play peculiar games.

In Leazes Terrace or Leazes Park
someone is loitering in the dark,
feeling the giggles rise in his throat
and fingering something under his coat.

He could be sidling along Forth Lane
to stop some girl from catching her train,
or stalking the grounds of the RVI
to see if a student nurse goes by.

In Belle Grove Terrace or Fountain Row
or Hunter's Road he's raring to go –
unless he's the quiet shape you'll meet
on the cobbles in Back Stowell Street.

Monk Street, Friars Street, Gallowgate
are better avoided when it's late.
Even in Sandhill and the Side
there are shadows where a man could hide.

So don't go lightly along Darn Crook
because the Ripper's been brought to book.
Wear flat shoes, and be ready to run:
remember, sisters, there's more than one.

Anne Stevenson

TELEVISION

Hug me, mother of noise,
Find me a hiding place.
I am afraid of my voice.
I do not like my face.

Jenny Joseph

THERE ARE MORE ACCIDENTS IN THE HOME
THAN ON THE ROADS

I remember hearing a story of a whole family
Destroyed in one go by a ring of a doorbell.
No, not electrocution, nor gun shot.
Like this:
The young mother was bathing the baby when
    the bell rang;
The toddler hastening to answer, fell down the
    stairs
Skull cracked on arrival; the mother ran to the
    screams;
The baby drowned.
It was a telegram, the door, to tell her
Her husband had been killed in an accident.

Well, old friend, this was your Northern humour
To bring, to pantomime level, such Greek disaster
Told in such a way I could disbelieve it.
But I thought of that dreadful tale when I heard
    this one:

A disappointed girl waited at home
Long past the days when he might possibly ring
The first man who'd said he would.

Heavy-hearted, empty, she dragged upstairs
And then, wild buzzing, the 'phone was actually
    ringing.
Frenzied, she dashed, and gasping picked it up
Ready with her joy. "Jane?" "Oh yes!"
"Would you like to suck my cock? It's a great
    big huge one."
Unlikely the stranger expected such blasts of
    tears.
Every time the 'phone rings she shakes with
    shame.

Fleur Adcock

THINGS

There are worse things than having behaved
    foolishly in public.
There are worse things than these miniature
    betrayals,
committed or endured or suspected; there are
    worse things
than not being able to sleep for thinking about
    them.
It is 5 a.m. All the worse things come stalking in
and stand icily about the bed looking worse
    and worse and worse.

Marilyn Hacker

TO IVA, TWO-AND-A-HALF

Little fat baby, as we
don't run the world, I
wince that I can't
drive a car or a truck, ice-
skate, build shelves and
tables, ride
you up five flights of
stairs on my shoulders.
I notice you noticing
who rides most of the Big
Motorcycles, drives buses,
stacks grocery cartons, makes
loud big holes in the street.
"Mustn't hit little girls!" meaning
you, though who'd
know if we didn't say so!
Soon they'll be telling you
you can't be
Batman, Shakespeare, President, or God.
Little fat baby, going on
schoolgirl, you can be
anyone, but it won't be
easy.

Adrienne Rich

TRANSLATIONS

You show me the poems of some woman
my age, or younger
translated from your language

Certain words occur: *enemy, oven, sorrow*
enough to let me know
she's a woman of my time

obsessed

with Love, our subject:
we've trained it like ivy to our walls
baked it like bread in our ovens
worn it like lead on our ankles
watched it through binoculars as if
it were a helicopter
bringing food to our famine
or the satellite
of a hostile power

I begin to see that woman
doing things: stirring rice
ironing a skirt
typing a manuscript till dawn

trying to make a call
from a phonebooth

The phone rings unanswered
in a man's bedroom
she hears him telling someone else
Never mind. She'll get tired—
hears him telling her story to her sister

who becomes her enemy
and will in her own time
light her own way to sorrow

ignorant of the fact this way of grief
is shared, unnecessary
and political

Gillian Allnutt

TWO SKETCHES
for Monica and Alice

I   **Hiroshima, 1945**

Kasa promises. She walks
carefully all the way back
from the shop.

She has one foot on the step
when the sun slips. Her shadow stops.
She looks up.

The sun
does not fall down
until late in the afternoon.

That is a promise. It has been
given to us.
It is only eight fifteen.

She is bringing a bottle of rice wine.
It is precious.
There will be a celebration.

The house is gone.
Kasa stops. There is a shadow on the step
looking up.

2   Birmingham, 1983

Alice examines the shadow
that lies before her
like a future.

It is fantastic:
an elegant woman dressed in black,
an old one bent over a stick.

Alice stops short.
She is only eight,
but she can just imagine it.

Alice, come on up.
The sun has reached the bottom of the step.
It is quarter past eight.

Tomorrow is
another day. That is a promise.
Come.

Alice forgets her shadow. Carelessly
it hops before her
two steps at a time.

Selima Hill

A VOICE IN THE GARDEN

Gerald's here! my mother called,
Are you ready? The taxi was waiting
to take us to our weekly swimming lessons.
I drove through Marylebone like a V.I.P.
our kind neighbour close beside me,
smelling of soap and peppermint . . .
He squatted on the edge of the pool
and shouted *One, two! One, two!* as I struggled
with the water like a kitten. I kept my eyes
on the gold buttons of his blazer.
They were as smooth and glossy
as the boiled sweets he liked to suck,
and offer to his young friends.
I sank and kicked and spat out water.
The bright buttons rose and fell . . .

And then one day he came in beside me,
his old grey body quaking
like a mollusc without its shell.
The wet wool of his bathing trunks
reminded me of blankets I had peed on.
His hands in the moving water
seemed to float between my legs.
He smiled. I swam to the edge of the pool
and pulled myself over the steps.
The heated water trickled down my legs
as I wrapped my towel round me, like a shawl.

That was our last swimming lesson,
but he still came to tea on Sundays,
after his 'little siesta',
and sat down in the seat next to mine.

As he listened to my mother –
picking his biscuits off his plate
with pink eager fingers, lifting
his tea-cup to his lips, and nodding –
he pressed a silver florin in my hand.
I kept them in a muff in my drawer,
under my uniform. At last I poured them
into a plastic bag and took them by bus
to The Little Sisters Of The Poor
in Albert Street . . . Next Sunday, I hid
in the garden, but he came pushing his way
through the roses, looking for me.
I heard the twigs breaking up, and his voice
in the bushes calling and calling –
Yoo-hoo, Gerald's here, yoo-hoo . . .

Carol Ann Duffy

WARMING HER PEARLS

Next to my own skin, her pearls. My mistress
bids me wear them, warm them, until evening
when I'll brush her hair. At six, I place them
round her cool, white throat. All day I think
 of her,

resting in the Yellow Room, contemplating silk
or taffeta, which gown tonight? She fans herself
whilst I work willingly, my slow heat entering
each pearl. Slack on my neck, her rope.

She's beautiful. I dream about her
in my attic bed; picture her dancing
with tall men, puzzled by my faint, persistent
   scent
beneath her French perfume, her milky stones.

I dust her shoulders with a rabbit's foot,
watch the soft blush seep through her skin
like an indolent sigh. In her looking-glass
my red lips part as though I want to speak.

Full moon. Her carriage brings her home. I see
her every movement in my head . . . Undressing,
taking off her jewels, her slim hand reaching
for the case, slipping naked into bed, the way

she always does . . . And I lie here awake,
knowing the pearls are cooling even now
in the room where my mistress sleeps. All night
    I feel their absence and I burn.

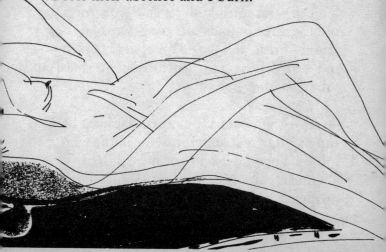

Jenny Joseph

WARNING

When I am an old woman I shall wear purple
With a red hat which doesn't go, and doesn't
    suit me.
And I shall spend my pension on brandy and
    summer gloves
And satin sandals, and say we've no money for
    butter.
I shall sit down on the pavement when I'm tired
And gobble up samples in shops and press alarm
    bells
And run my stick along the public railings
And make up for the sobriety of my youth.
I shall go out in my slippers in the rain
And pick the flowers in other people's gardens
And learn to spit.

You can wear terrible shirts and grow more fat
And eat three pounds of sausages at a go
Or only bread and pickle for a week
And hoard pens and pencils and beermats and
    things in boxes.

But now we must have clothes that keep us dry
And pay our rent and not swear in the street
And set a good example for the children.
We must have friends to dinner and read the
    papers.

But maybe I ought to practise a little now?
So people who know me are not too shocked and surprised
When suddenly I am old, and start to wear purple.

Vicki Feaver

THE WAY WE LIVE

In rooms whose lights
On winter evenings
Make peepshows of our lives –

Behind each window
A stage so cluttered up
With props and furniture

It's not surprising
We make a mess of what began
So simply with *I love you*.

Look at us: some
Slumped in chairs
And hardly ever speaking

And others mouthing
The same tired lines to ears
That long ago stopped listening.

Once we must have dreamed
Of something better.
But even those who swapped

One partner for another
Have ended up
Just like the rest of us:

Behind doors, moving outside
Only to go to work
Or spend weekends with mother.

Lauris Edmond

WELLINGTON LETTER XV

All this week
I was sick,
last month I suffered
constant headaches,
earlier I broke my arm
and it was slow to heal.
In time my children will die
and their children
and it will be as though
I had never lived;
but the earth will remain,
these delicate willows
touching the river water
will pass through perpetual summers
and women I shall not know
will walk among their trailing
scarves of silk, papery and green.

Frances Horovitz

WILSON WARD

earless
eyeless
noseless
we drift on
in our lonely beds
the old one
Mrs Rivers
eighty five
floats out
sans everything

*Written in hospital in August 1983: 'that's all
I can manage at the moment.'*

Carol Rumens

A WOMAN OF A CERTAIN AGE

'This must have been my life
but I never lived it.'
—Her childishly wide stare
at some diminishing reel
of space and brightness, half
illusory, half not,
stuns to an epitaph.
And I can read it all:
how a little lie
whitened to twenty years;
how she was chosen by
something called happiness,
yet nothing, nothing was hers.
And now she has to turn
away, and her bruised eyes
are smiling in their nets:
'It's simple, isn't it?
Never say the yes
you don't mean, but the no
you always meant, say that,
even if it's too late,
even if it kills you.'

Author Index